# Vines of Life

by
Julie A. Jennings

First Edition

Published in the United States of America

MoonMist Publishing
P.O. Box 1672
Fredericksburg, VA 22402

ISBN 978-0-615-25357-2

Cover illustration by David Jennings

# TABLE OF CONTENTS

## Table of Contents

Acknowledgements

I would like to honor the people who were instrumental in getting my poetry book published.

My son, David, for his part in designing the book cover that is so fitting to the title. I appreciate the long and hard work of my editor, publisher and dear friend, June Diehl, who always showed me why something did or didn't work.

I give my appreciation to two friends, Jill Behe for her sound advice and listening to many poems and to Rae Banks for her patience, advice, and for sitting hour after hour listening to each poem as I read it aloud and pointing out where changes were needed.

I want to honor the support and revision advice of my writers group, Writers In Action, and to all the people in my past that have been my encouragement towards this endeavor.

My special thanks to my mom, my sister, and my brother for their profound belief in me.

Last but not least, my heartfelt thanks to the support of my family who gave me time and space to work so I could finish Vines of Life and to my husband who also helped with the cover of the book.

Julie A. Jennings

# ROAD TO COUNTRY

# FALSE PARADISE

Play your little games, play your little guitar,
squeeze me; dance me into the dark sorrow,
drive me away; drive me into insanity,
feel the teardrops of pain; let me go,
into the jet of another tomorrow.

Don't give me those tiffany diamonds,
sweating the big time isn't for me,
instead listen to the music of my heartstrings,
hear despair singing through the sky
darkness rides into my soul, my heart.

Memories shared are now marred,
was so sure we'd make it, baby
the sun has gone down on our love,
into a flood gate of tearstained heart
so just go and hang onto your little gal,

And let those kisses be untrue,
you are just a country boy liar,
who has handed me a river of pain,
tell me where we went astray.

Down the country road of hell,
you played me for a fool,
swept me into false paradise,
struck down into its depths.

Baby, you promised me the moon,
we gazed upon the falling stars.
Why should it matter so?
Years of crimson lies,
There is nothin' left of love.

# COUNTRY CHRISTMAS FAIR

Remember that old country Christmas fair?
The time when I drank all that German beer?
We rode the merry ground of love that night,
and we tasted the kisses of sweet cotton candy.

Held hands, laughing, running through the rain,
delighting, tasting the excitement of love,
swept into the artwork of our own lives,
country music playing our song.

Our hearts wrapped up in each other,
like a winning blue ribbon prize,
a recipe of sweetened love,
and we ride them horses, manes a flying.

Country hats flapping in that wind,
you are my man, and I'm your woman,
dancing to the heartbeat of love,
satin wind touches the deep of my soul.

We go on home and you fix me supper,
afterwards we go onto the porch,
eatin' ice cream, and chewing bubblegum,
portions of memory on days gone by.

Remember that old country Christmas fair?
The time I drank all that German beer.
we played and won the game of love,
the light in your eyes just for me.

**Julie A. Jennings**

# BITTER CUP OF LOVE

Twasn't it yesterday that we shared a cup of Joe by the campfire?
The harvest moon lit up the night sky as we made love
in the open and wide spaces past old Branson's farm.
The chilly wind didn't matter for we had the warmth of love.

There were no holes in the fences as we held each other,
then she came in her fancy cowboy hat and boots,
holding onto you like she held onto her beer,
Bitter wind soaked through me as I stood in shock.

Now I can really use that cup of Joe by the campfire,
the fence, my heart has many holes,
cowboy with her at your side and me discarded,
these holes won't be mended,
so I'll hop on down to our old fishing hole.

Fish will tug on the pole, the way she tugged my heart,
A school of pain swims through me,
I pick up my cup of joe, looking into it's murky depth,
the fire warms my body, my heart still empty, cold,
she warms his body with her melting kisses.
Our memory, our love, a forgotten fishing hole.

# UNDER THE APPLE TREE

I was driving my Chevy down the dusty country road,
and I saw her on the left walking like she was something,
hair in one of those high ponytails decorated like,
my window down, arm hanging out,
the gal singing one of them fine country tunes.

My heart melting like sugar in summer's heat,
I knew then she was the woman for me,
parkin' I offer her a ride down the road,
and  give her my love, my heart and life.

I was driving my Chevy down the dusty country road,
and I saw her on the left walking like she was something,
hair in one of those high ponytails decorated like,
my window down, arm hanging out,
the gal singing one of them fine country tunes.

We were poorer than the proverbial church mice,
but richer than the richest country homes,
sitting next to me under the old apple tree.
I wipe her tears feeling her sadness under my skin,
so I tell her ride those worries away.

I was driving my Chevy down the dusty country road,
and I saw her on the left walking like she was something,
hair in one of those high ponytails decorated like,
my window down, arm hanging out,
the gal singing one of them fine country tunes.

Don't let life slip slide you off the horse,
she smiles, lips pink as the wild rose,
smells of sweet green apples waft by,
as she takes my hand into hers, she said,
we got a whole lot of sunshine,
even with the torrential pours,
our love is a mountain of country riches.

I was driving my Chevy down the dusty country road,
and I saw her on the left walking like she was something,
hair in one of those high ponytails decorated like,
my window down, arm hanging out,
the gal singing one of them fine country tunes.

She's the song in the wind and my heart,
walking hand in hand, down the old dusty road,
moonlight and stars peek on out,
the cattle are bawling loud and low,
our love brought us our darlin's,
twins, a boy and a girl with a slight curl,
born from those times underneath the apple tree.

I was driving my Chevy down the dusty country road,
and I saw her on the left walking like she was something,
hair in one of those high ponytails decorated like,
my window down, arm hanging out,
the gal singing one of them fine country tunes.

# VINES OF LIFE

# DETERMINATION

Skyline of hope reaches across the horizon,
Templates of emotions rise and fall,
Like the changing of seasons,
Twilight's success is driven,
through the prairies of
determination.

# COMEDY

Comedy an enlightenment to life itself,
the realism verses
the encampment
of imagination.
Suspense travels its'
paths of laughter.
A gift that frees weighty
tensions of today's life.

# STAIRWELL

Hiding in the shadow of my life,
the sun peeps out,
and closes again.
Trials of fortitude,
deliberating on the open door,
a lighted emblem shows the way,
illuminating each darkened hall in
the stairwell of my mind.

# UNITED IN DESPAIR

(In memory of Sept 11, 2001)

Gusting wind like child's play
swirls a blaze of colors to the ground.
Resplendent like a tree of hope.
Brushed heartache of despair;
Deliberate force explodes.
Impact shocks
thickets of injury and death.

Clear skyline crimson,
like an ill made Lego building;
towers collapse.
Bruised hearts united
primed for battle.
Cascade of leaves
bury the debris
tainted in autumn's treachery.

**Julie A. Jennings**

# A DREAM CAME TRUE

Long ago a dream came true,
a child was born and that
was you.

Long ago a dream came true,
a toddler brightened my days,
and that was you.

Long ago, a dream came true,
a child small and shy,
would hug me,
and that was you.

Long ago, a dream came true,
a child growing,
imploding into wonder,
and that was you.

Long ago, a dream came true,
a child of God,
stood on the steps,
reverent,
and that was you.

Long ago, a dream came true,
a teen of caring,
held me tight,
and that was you.

Today, I want a dream come true,
a young man of success,
to bear me proud,
let it be you.

# ONCE IN A LIFE-TIME

In honor of Val Dummond


Once in a lifetime a person comes along,
leading us to the rainbow of our dreams.
She facilitates the heart of our songs,
sharpening the joyous beaming
of our imagination as we write.
It is you through the years
that has given us hope and delight.
Today is a celebration of life,
a joyous moment in starlight.
A carnival time to share
in your seventy-fifth birthday.
You have the gracious flair
of giving to us all your love.
Now we extend our hand and hearts,
to you, the woman who will
always be a great part
of our lives at the Writer's
Roundtable.

Happy Seventy-Fifth Birthday.

Love, Julie Jennings

# ROSE OF LIFE

I'm crying trying to reach you,
and your heart is locked,
into the dungeons of drugs.
I'm sobbing,
not knowing what to say,
tears are in my eyes,
the rose of life is waiting,
but you choose the thorns,
it is lonely here.
In the heart of not understanding,
success waits for you on a pathway,
and you choose the false road.
I want to hold you tight,
take away the pain you hold,
but there are walls you've built,
unhealthy secrets that you hold.
Don't you see us crying?
Wanting the best for you?
We are crying, trying to reach you.
Inside my mind whirls,
with what we can do.
Don't turn away from
the love we have for you.
Dreams remembered,
dreams forgotten,
in a land of nowhere.
I'm crying trying to reach you,
unlock your heart from
the dungeons of drugs.
Key in to the success
waiting for you.
Tears are in my eyes,
the rose of life is waiting.

# TERRAIN OF LIFE
# FORCES

# PRECIPICE

In our fountain of youth,
we know all.
Our struggle to adulthood
standing on the precipice to life,
believing in eternal invincibility
as we question who we are.

# STOLEN THRILL

Stolen thrill
runs a vein
spurting
blood
scouting
cars
caught
in
stolen thrill,
gun resounds
echoes of life
are what's left
from
youth's
stolen thrill.

# ANCIENT FRIEND

Worn wrinkles upon your face,
an ancient friend,
where hopes began,
my diary.

# WRESTLING MATCH

Deep in the soul of my heart is a warmth that I must cover with ice, an ice
so strong that the warmth can't break through. Divisions of life are
crushing me, bruising the mother's love. I walk in the dark. There will never
be the light that I've looked for. There is nothing but sorrow deepening in
the caverns of my soul.

Unrest ravels each part of me; I wrestle with the angels and the devils. I
reach for joy, light and love, but they are just beyond my reach. Great rivers
of sadness befall me as tears drip, then fall like a water over rocks.

The beauty escapes me. Life's hope, my dreams dissipated. My past and my
future rest in darkness. Be Still. I command my heart and it goes at a fast
pace like no other. Why? The inflictions of pain are greater than a blade
cutting through my heart, severing it into pieces.

# COMFORT

Soft as cotton,
a tiny wail emits,
growing louder,
smell of baby powder.
Tired eyes,
louder cries,
comfort lounging
in a rocking chair.
Music to the ears
as baby shudders
last cries,
falling into the
solemn dusk
of sleep.

# THE HAUNTING

There are souls deep in the caverns of the mountain,
dripping vivid blood, eerie thoughts scream
echoing, sweeping haunted cries.
There are souls deep in the caverns of the mountains.
So in the night, in deepest sleep,
dreams of the lost will haunt your night.

# JANA

I hear you on the shore, my dear of another land,
swishing satin on white tipped waves.
You were my love, the sweetheart of my life,
now you belong to another who owns the deep.
Neptune has swept you into his arms,
Jana, I bid you adieu.

# LIFTED

Are you really that unfeeling? Giving me the thorns of your disdain?
Treating me with the soft sulfur of a lying tongue.
What is it that I've done in your life to be treated so low?
It is your adultery in your heart that's caused our love to break.
I offered you the warm fire of love. You turned away. Our dreams
shattering like the seven year curse of a broken mirror.
What could have been-will never be. I walk into an unknown
future knowing anything would be better than the past.

# SOLITARY FAMILY LOST

I walk the solitary line of a family lost,
rainbows shine in whimsical mockery,
it is hell's downward spiral,
as I hang by a golden thread.

My ears are ringing with sorrow,
of things that could have been,
a child lies on my heart,
I'm suffocating in the putrid air.

Time has slowed like a turtle's crawl,
each step taken, all forsaken,
the earth vibrates underneath my feet,
flames missile toward my soul.

Each ache an agonizing uprising,
light switches to dark,
my body is at war,
with none other than myself.

# ILLUSIONS

Sky full of ink,
the stars seem to wink,
a moon of yellow gold,
are illusions to behold.

# CURTAIN

Tears curtain down her face,
twisted years of hope entwined,
tiptoeing in the hot coals of emotion.
Stain of desire tightly bound,
tears cleanse her despair.

# HOPE

**H**appy
**O**de
**P**eace
**E**njoyment.

# HOPES AND DREAMS

Success is what I wished for each child.
Now, I have a son who is wild,
fraught with the tension of his deceit
afraid his sins will he only repeat.

Hardened soul, hardened heart,
blackened like chimney soot.
No cares, no fares,
the circus of life remains.

The fears of family hit the core,
hurts, tears and pain spread
like the plague of old,
just as damaging.

Prayer balances the soul,
meditation holds my hand,
as I explore the terrain,
of hope and dreams.

# WISHES

In the shadows,
a young man
stands by the railing
waiting to be noticed.
His life is meandering and hailing;
he's learning to be focused.
My dreams are of his success,
a life of hope singled his way.
I wish this from my deep solar plexus.

# GRADUATION

A new day is dawning
for my senior year is ending,
life awaits us taunting,
for the years ahead impending.

# SONG

Music is a joy,
relaxing me, calming me,
why can't we employ
our music more frequently?

# TEARS

**T**ormented
**E**motions
**A**lways
**R**aging
**S**ilently.

# VANITY

Strutting like a peacock,
reaching for a comb,
stroking down her hair
in the face of vanity.

# TO DREAM

To dream of a star
the impossible dream,
to reach so far
for the milky cream.

Climbing the mountains
in search for a star,
where glittering mountains,
lay completely unmarred.

A star so exquisitely rare,
the search is long
hunting for this ware
which time prolongs.

To dream of a star,
the impossible dream,
to reach so far
for the milky cream.

Julie A. Jennings

# SUNNYSIDE UP

# THE OCEAN

Fiery red, fierce yellows,
brighten blue horizon,
color spills through the sky,
heightened waves beat their foam,
against the jagged cliffs.
Salty sea air rushes through,
grey seagull dives for fish,
sunset invokes peace,
settling down for night.

# FALL'S WALTZ

There is a chill in the air, as I face the moon,
a sign that rustic leaves will fall soon.
They will sway in the breeze, a waltz to the ground,
the dance will end without a sound.
Pine and Great Oak limbs tremble,
thunder belches in the sky,
people and animals scurry to assemble,
winter's white coat is nigh.
As I face the moon and shiver,
teardrops fall from the sky,
streaming from leaves like a river,
there is a chill in the air, as I face the moon.
A sign that rustic leaves will waltz soon.

# MUSIC'S DELIGHT

The music is delightful,
solemn and caressing,
each note like nightfall,
swept into the sea of stars.

# ONCE AGAIN

Haloed angels dust the ground with white,
feel the golden warmth of fires lit.
After walking in the chill of night,
melodies of Christmas emit,
into families celebrations,
and Church congregations,
reverent thoughts of Christ's birth,
Christmas dances its' mirth,
once again.

# TIMELESS

Lush green jungles
anticipating an adventure
to clear, incandescent waters,
descending through the
mossy warmth,
to the beauty of lapping
waves.
The smell of the salted sea,
holds an array of kaleidoscope
fish,
swimming in the clear,
tepid waters
of Guam.

# TRINITY ROSE

Sweet, playful and a
bundle of delight.
Chocolate chip eyes
bright with curiosity,
dancing feet twirling,
swirling,
a rainbow of fun.
Dipping into the
creativity of life.
Warmth of snuggle hugs,
walks in the park
even at dark.
Running, sliding
love abiding
Trinity, my granddaughter
a bundle of delight.

# BLANKET

What is summer,
I thought,
glorious blanket of flowers,
and warmth of sun
covering
country hills.

# RANCH LIFE

The horse grazes in the flower fields,
and the cows are milked at sunrise,
farmers wipe sweat from their brow,
plowing the fertile ground into harvest.

# ORDINANCE OF HEART

The scrawny man knew, the forbidden rule,
of adultery's temptation, fruit of his heart,
the elation of his sin, led to his downfall.

# DIVISIONS

The seasons now descend,
into a warming trend,
dividing winter into spring,
as birds enchantingly sing.

# EDGE

Rust leaves, tinges of red,
designed with lines of life,
light upon shade
curling into the edge of winter.

# GLASS REFLECTIONS

The river still as night,
reflected light
like stars
with pin pointed wishes
and glass reflections,
I wish
and truth is
revealed.

# LAST PAGE

Sun through the trees glitter rays
in all its might and glory,
nestled in the yellow rose petals,
sweetened with the dewdrop
of summer's last page.

# NATURE AT PLAY

Birds stand at the precipice
seeking a handout from
the ocean's divine hand
whip cream tops the surf,
gray green waves devour the sand.

# BLANKET OF FOG

Golden wheat colored grass,
buried in the sandy silt,
golden sun smiles on the beach,
blades of tall green grass
ever so watchful in the breeze,
as a thick whiteness rolls in.

# THE PHOTOGRAPHER

A man stands in the quiet wind,
intense, observing each detail,
sand, grass and driftwood.
His tripod isolated
in the realm of drifting dreams.

**Julie A. Jennings**

# FISHING SOLITUDE

Children busy with toys,
Divinity couldn't stand the noise,
she left the tykes with husband Mike,
at Mystic Lake,
fog settles in, fishing pole in hand,
a trout is caught
in that spot.
A moment of fishing solitude.

# THE SHADOW AND ME

Out in the meadow
I see,
a small shadow,
imitating me,
when I skip, it skips,
free
running, running around
a tree,
the shadow it follows me.

# MORNING

Pink rosy sunrise,
blanketing the mountain
with your dewy
cloud aired fountains
in a spring morning.

# THE KITE

The sky diver gains
altitude
past all clouds
reaching into the blue
heavens.
It's string unwinds
wildly
as the wind
blows fiercely
breaking it's string.
The wind pulls
hard
making the kite
twist
around large trees.

# MEMORIES

Going back in days of
time
flipping coins and silver
dimes,
watching birds in the
sky
wishing that I could
fly.
Singing songs of dreamful
play,
making things out of clay.
Ahh, to be a child
again,
and play in the forests
glen.

**Julie A. Jennings**

# DREAMS AND MAGICAL THINGS

The light sweetened fragrant breeze,
fairies of make believe,
a child's starlit face,
sweetened with God's grace,
the spring of a gentle rain,
sprinkling on my window pane,
and the brilliant smile of the sun,
makes life ever so fun.

Fluffy white clouds peeping
from grayish shrouds,
magical moments skating,
memories that are fading.
Walks among the ocean blue waves,
golden dreams to pass the days,
and flowers softly swaying
bent in quiet praying.

The snowflakes falling array,
colors of the blue jay,
sunset at summers eve,
silvery webs that spiders weave,
mountains topped with fresh snow
while faces beam aglow,
wheat that shines like brass,
these I do not disdain,
it is my magical claim.

# MYTHICAL AND PHILOSPHICAL

# FLIGHT

Her name was Pandora: Without color, or shame
she opened the fabled box against her misgivings.
The battle of her conscience: A crusade against God.
A herd of evil fleeing, into the night's gateway,
to a fresh spring morning, from an imprisoned box,
swift dying of earth, like the bird eating the worm,
land and sea, the evil spreads.

# RESONANCE OF PAST

Feudal wars have brought destruction
exploiting the castle lands,
flashing flames through fire swords,
jousting silver knights gleam in shades of honesty and shame
vying for the fair ladies hand,
through strength of show and bloodstained sword.
Deliverance of destruction shown through tapestries
In ornamental halls.

# THE GOD'S LITAGATION

On the wings of spring,
buds the cherry blossom tree,
sprawling sunset pink,
thoroughfares of life,
spreading good cheer
into every street of rift.

It is classical say the Greek Neophytes,
to become a god in the green pastures,
and raise their honor in flights of fancy,
knee bent, will bend in sad dismay.
It is the grievous torn blights
that wrenches the hearts of the Masters.

As they see the destructive play,
earths green reality, perishing.
Maybe they will grant us clemency.
Head bowed, knees bent in supplication,
entrenched in the sorrows of earths reality,
enmeshed into the gods' minds, our litigation.

Our hearts entwine, entangle
into the ropes of love,
rodeo stars ride the sky,
galloping into the moonlit-night,
enmeshed into the rodeo-ride
of eternal love-brightened love.

Rose petal ashes strewn about,
sweet smells trampled,
my heart is crumpled
into the cloying doubt.
Walking down the garden path,
stumbling over hurtful words
in ever seeding wrath,
pecking like the birds.
Where is the wonder in the air?
The sweet-dewed kisses, and
gentle touch of natures care?

# JOURNEY

I can see a silhouette,
a ship from afar,
waves so surly,
where does it journey?

A ghost ship traveling,
in the realms of time.
Is something else unraveling
as the sun glints gold?

Can you hear the sailor calling?
Gray fog rolls in,
the ship sinks in surly waves,
an ocean voyage to the deep.

The sailor's call from below,
a haunting, hollow sound
fills the chilly air,
daunting, challenging
the surly waves.

# BEWARE

Many ships have been lost,
struggling through tossing waves,
feeding the need for sacrifice,
danger in the ocean's beauty.

# EXPECTATION

We sail through the sea of hope,
engaging in the promises of life,
engulfed in our faded painted thoughts.

# ICE OBSERVATION

I look out from my cave of ice,
and see the dawning of an enterprise,
the world's science reaching,
people are beseeching
to be a part of the New World.

Across the sea of ice,
I see people gnawing like mice,
Trying to escape totalitarianism
As they seek to be part of
The New World of Utopia.

Their eyes are glazed with hope,
and they blindly grope,
to loosen their binds,
and free their avarice minds.

# REACHING

Fountains of youth prevail,
while the old watch
to no avail,
but wisdom reaches out,
to the young and old
and prevails.

# WARM SUN, WARM HEARTS

The warmth of the sun
is how warm our heart's
should be
we will have won
Then the right to be free.

Julie A. Jennings

# LAVA OF ROMANCE

# BUDDING LOVE

Sweet taste upon my lips,
the honeydew of
every kiss,
delighting, cherishing,
sunshine, warming, nourishing
our budding love together.

# TREASURE VAULT

In the velvet night
lie secrets of the heart,
held in the treasure
vault of stars.

# LOVE

Soft as a gentle breeze,
he whispers in my ear,
a feather tickle of
I love you.

# VELVET NIGHT

His touch, a moment of cherishment,
a healing of rifting pain,
as a chain of stars jewel the sky,
velvet night encases our love.

# ENTWINED

Red roses sweep through the garden,
sweet Gardenia scents the air,
grape vines entwined the house,
our hearts become one.

# CHERISH

Fluted glass, red wine fills its house
sparkling in rainbow window light,
waiting for lips first kiss,
savoring, flavoring gentle touch,
translucent, elusions, superior.

Sweet taste of lips to mine.
tingles down my spine.
Sparkles in my heart,
savoring the smoothness,
caressing my throat.

# ENCHANTMENT

The two walk the crest of ocean beach,
stars illustrate the sky like diamonds,
soft sand silk between their toes,
waves slather over their feet.

Deep contours in driftwood,
etched like the love in their heart,
gentle wind trails by,
sailor's ships sailing into sunset.

# GARDEN OF LOVE

I could feel the blazing heat tormenting my mind
melting in the sizzling passion of your arms,
burning my soul with grief's brand
the sword of love plunges deep into my heart,
stabs of pain create an agony mixed with love.
Bleeding heart, flower of my soul delivered into my spirit.
Petals of time faded into a laconic memory,
misted thoughts drift slowly like a fragrant garden,
but as seasons change, so do the flowers of love.
The lush of summer green has changed to fall.
Colors of time fall from the recesses of memory.
Branches of love laden with snow
break into the crisp air, crunching a bit of soul.
A drift of snow hills has buried our memories
Until Spring thaws the garden path of love
our love will remain frozen underneath the hurts.
Is that the fragrant breeze of spring delivering
a warming trend of hope on my heart of love swept
under the crisp snow hills, peeking flowers of hope and memories,
budding into the full bloom of summer's promise.
Scented with the memories and passions of time
we won't allow our love to become a myth of sunshine buried.
Instead our love will begin fresh like a fragrant garden
given the proper nourishment and care.
It will flourish with the tenderness given
and again in the summer heat; I will feel the sizzle of your passion
as you wrap your arms around me, cherishing and nurturing
the fragility of love's emotions before the petals fall again.

# SAFE

Paint me into a cave of love,
sheltering our kisses from the rain,
waves of wind course through the sky,
and we are safe in each other's arms,
away from the yawning of winter's snow.

# LIGHT

Her auburn curls crested in the wind.
Was there a heaven and a hell?
Only God could tell.

She sought a haven to keep sorrow,
from stinging her heart,
Would love come to her tomorrow?
Shadows cast no light.

She ached yet stood like the oak,
drawing strength from dawning sun,
filtering her great pain,
into a cloak of hope.

# IMAGE

The lamplight glows from the ghostly house,
rubbled streets glisten from new fallen rain,
gray blue colonial home in its haunted past.
Windows open its wondering eyes,
into the hearts of pain and love, past and present.
A haunted melody of life's refrain.

# PAINTED

Morning sunrise dawns,
its face peeps in nights shroud,
dewdrops sparkle.
Jeweled teardrops glisten.
I realize I've been conned.
Marriage painted bright,
beneath bright covers
lies a hurtful heart
cloaked in darkness.
Pain is within the painted sunrise.

# MY LOVE

I tremble in anticipation of your touch,
the comfort of your heart
beating next to mine.
Didatic motions of love
whisper in your gentle voice
I tremble in you,
my love.

# MATRIMONY

In the solace of comforting arms,
cheered by your animated charm.
My heart sweetened with engaging words,
captured in love's fidelity.
Through the craggy jets of life,
tranquil jewels sparkle.
A kiss seals my acceptance
of love's marriage dance.

# RED

Red silk curtains tied with gold nestled
against the blue-gray ocean,
sweeping waves licked onto land,
an egret folds it's wings watching
two lovers eating an apple,
their passion palpable, and as
far reaching as the red sunset.

In the distance, red birds sing,
melodies sweetening the earths core,
A chill courses through the air,
pillowed on the ground
are the slender red flames
warming their hands and hearts
in their newfound valentine.

Nearby red roses perfume the sky,
the lovers rest in each others arms,
she dreamt of cherries, sweet
and tasty like their kisses.
Night has fallen, the flames die down,
but their love has risen into passion.

# PASSION

Your look of gentle excitement,
the fiery passion of your touch
brings a new enlightment,
that I now must clutch.

In tenderness we touch,
your cheek against mine,
our arms entwined
in a lover's embrace.

From you I have learned,
how passions arise
as our wheels turn
in a lover's enterprise.

# SOLACE OF LOVE

I wrap myself in the warmth of sunshine
radiating in his love and camaraderie,
sitting together in the solace
of love.

# ROMANCE

The fire blazes warmth
in the room adding to the
delight of a valentine couple's
romantic night.

Julie A. Jennings

# SPIRITUAL

# MOTION

God's warmth reflects on the sand
and water
like silver diamonds in the wind
sifting, creating,
artist in constant motion.

# WARMTH

God reaches out his hand, imploring,
as my heart goes exploring,
His merciful love soft as sand,
enduring, strong like the ocean,
I feel the warmth of his emotion.
Kelp moves in the sea, waiting,
for a special landing,
God moves like the clouds, waiting,
for our prayers, love and devotion
we land in his outstretched arms.
There is no denying of his affection.

# DIVINITY

A river streams and people dream
like the silence of the night,
stars reflecting light,
dancing sparkles
swimming in the warmth
of God's divine love.

# RELEASE

God houses in our hearts,
if we so choose,
training us in his way,
delivering us from sorrows.

Swaddling us in his love,
giving us dreams,
and immense hope,
delivering us from sorrow.

# CREATION

The sunrise is a harvest of color,
gold, oranges and reds blend morning.
Below an ocean of cresting foam,
dark blue greens coast over orange sand,
God's beauty drawn in simplicity.
The sunrise ocean.

# TOMORROW'S DREAMS

Laughter trickles through the soul
drowning out the sorrows,
giving dreams of new tomorrows.

# GOD'S QUILT

Can you see the eagles flying?
The stars in the sky gliding?
Precious gems sparkle the sand
these are the handiwork
of God.
The surf crashes over hardened rocks,
barnacles cling for their lives.
Tempestuous storms,
normalcy for those who live by the
ocean
God's handiwork quilted into life.

# THE STROLL

I appreciate the warmth in my soul,
as I carry my thoughts
in God's walk of life.
Pitter Patter of little feet,
chitter chatter of voices,
radiating in the sun.
Troubles washed away by
serenity's heartstrings.
The lake sings to me of happiness.

Green buds spring forth
on bare branches,
pine trees and evergreens
reach for a crowning sky,
Mallard ducks swoosh
through rippling the lake,
while geese sing song
in a cloudless sky.

A small boy throws bread
to the birds, smiling, laughing,
people walk their dogs
as seagulls coast by.
Twinges of spring are here today,
children play and run
with their ball in the field.
A day of blessing brought to my heart.

# MY GIRL

She is small, delicate and walks in the air of love,
her heart is big like the sun and just as warm.
Laughter fills her soul like a bubbling brook,
simple things, fishing, running, and flying a kite
are the desires that sing through her and she
is dusted with the sparkles of life.
Dynamite in God's love.

# MIRROR OF LIFE

A river flows caressing the gray stones,
bleeding hearts carve into the silt.
Lines of trees, sensuous in the sunlight,
a mirror of life into tears and laughter.

Deep crevices crack my heart,
happiness sweeps into willow tears,
sweeping the ground of light,
still the river swims of great hope.

# SUGAR SWEET

# REMEMBER

Remember the jingle of your mother's necklace
as you tried it on? Eyes furtive, heart beating quick.
Remember digging in the mud, putting sticks, rocks
and weeds in a bucket and calling it stew? The surprised
look that your mother gave you when you really wanted
her to taste this invention?
Remember the trips to the beach, small toes snuggled
in the sand?  Warmth filling your body as you built
the sandcastles only to watch it be flooded. Tear filled eyes
and mommy hugs were the only comforting blanket.
Remember that stolen piece of candy from her drawer
and the strings of guilt that were attached with that action?
There is none other than the power of a mother's love.
Remember always her unconditional hugs and forgiveness
that swept your tears away much like the ocean with
the sandcastles. Remember. Always. My mom.

# UNIVERSE OF DELIGHT

There is a star in my life and she shines bright,
her eyes shine with newfound love
cradling her own little bundle
with large round eyes that scan details
and talk with gurgling smiles.
There is a star in my life and she shines bright.
My daughter is a star and to add to the
generations of stars is my granddaughter, Annalisa.

# FRIENDSHIP

True friends are golden and no matter
what happens, they are there in the thick of the
woods or in the constellations of happiness.
They encourage each step and when
necessary remind you of what you need to do.
They are there in the face of adversity,
and sweep you in their arms encouragingly.
Friends show you how it is and still wrap
their love around you like a big Christmas present.

# ENCHANTING

Have you ever wondered why birds fly? Or seen the enraptured look
of an infant and wished you could look at the world anew, again?
In the silent of the night, you can hear the magic, a world of creativity spins
in your head like an old fashioned top.

Imagination twines itself within your soul and the words pick up a peppy
conversation. Infants are magical with their wonderment and the muse is
magical as it lets you hear the music of creativity.

Have you ever wondered why birds fly? Delve into your soul and meet
the muse of magical words. Fly like a bird on wings of imagination, create
the wonderment of a newborn. Spin into births of new stories. Enjoy the
muse.

# THE DELIVERY

I sit on the porch listening for the jingle of the ice-cream
man. Small hands clench the dime waiting for his white
truck to bring fudgicles, and popsicles. Flavors of the
rainbow. Delighting taste buds on a warm summers eve.
Instead a man dressed in white brings milk up the
cement sidewalk whistling a happy tune. With a smile
and a hello, he lifts the silver lid to the container
setting the milk bottles inside. I smile but tears quiver
disappointed that the delivery was the milkman.
Wait. I see his truck. Smiling with joy, I race toward
the Popsicle man. He stops and asks which flavor
suits my fancy. A fudgicle. Already I feel the cool
chocolate dripping down my chin, melting in my
mouth. Of course, he says. Your favorite. He leaves
and other children run after him for their share of
summer. I delight in the reward of my chase.

# GRAND THINGS

Sing to me of great things and a love so great
that no love can surpass it. Sing to me of the highest
mountain illuminating glory and sunshine. No love
can surpass it. Sing to me of valleys and hills. Beautiful,
majestic, but His love is greater than all of these.
He is majestic, glorious like the sun, He is Beautiful,
His love surpasses all. Our God, Almighty.

# BEAUTIFUL EXPRESSION

Poetry a thing within my soul,
a happy or sorrowing song,
to help my emotions feel full.
Some are short, some are long.
Each has a special meaning.
It's a land of growing greening.
A soothing, soothing, lotion,
to my mind under stress.
Its thoughts floating within,
wanting beautiful expression.

# SPLENDOR

There is a song in my heart
when I hear the robins and blue jays.
There is a beauty to impart as I
view the meadows, daisies and riverbeds.
There is a dance in the wind as clouds
move through the sky.
There is a lilt in my voice
as love of life
enters my soul.

Julie A. Jennings

# HAIKU

# LAMENTATION

A willow weeping
as the rain squalls from the storm,
umbrellas protect.

# DRAPED

Children kneel by bedside
hands folded, heads bowed, reverent
wrapped in God's snug arms.

# VICTORY

The lake ripples gentle,
white swans grace the elegance
triumphant peace dawns.

# ENCOURAGEMENT

Inspiring swan
from gray down into beauty
reminder of hope.

# MYSTICAL

There is a howling
in the moonlight snow
mystery of ancient.

# HEART OF THE MATTER

The soul deepens red
Sin scatters like rose petals
Defying the truth.

# JULIE'S BIO

The muse has been with Julie since she was nine years old. In high school she wrote short stories, poems, and started a novella.

During her young married years, she joined a writing group to enhance her writing. When members were given "The Torn Blue Shirt" assignment, most of the group, much older than the author, wrote about mending the shirt. Julie challenged the story with a mystery involving a bloody torn shirt swept down from the river. Ever since, she has had a love of writing fiction.

She completed 50,050 word of her novel Glacier Creek, during the month of November 2004.

**Frost Dragons** is her current novel-in-progress.

**The Sun Never Rises, A Rainthology** published a short story and several poems.

A second anthology - **Dreammakers** came out June 2004, publishing several of her short stories and poetry.

Julie has been a facilitator of writing groups and currently teaches writing classes online.

The author lives in Washington State with her husband, who is retired Navy. She has three grown children, three grandchildren, and cats and a dog.

Her favorite activities besides writing and playing with her grandchildren are swimming, walking, crocheting, traveling, painting ceramics, raku, and photography. Her favorite place to visit is the ocean.